If God be with us,
there is no-one else left to fear

Nihil Obstat

P.J. Tynan, STD, Censor Theol. Deput.

Imprimatur

+ Gulielmus J. Walsh,
Archiepiscopus Dubliniensis Hiberniae Primas.

If God be with us

The Maxims of St Philip Neri

arranged for every day of the year by

Father F.W. Faber

GRACEWING

First published in 1994
Reprinted in 2004

Gracewing
2 Southern Avenue, Leominster
Herefordshire HR6 0QF

ISBN 0 85244 296 3

St Philip Neri

Contents

Preface

St Philip Neri (1515–1595) is known as the Apostle of Rome and the founder of the Congregation of the Oratory. It was thought fitting to re-issue the translation of his maxims and sayings (with slight corrections and notes) to pay tribute to the work of Fr Faber, who published his version in 1847 at St Wilfrid's Cheadle.

Readers should bear in mind that St Philip was writing in the sixteenth century and his spirituality speaks to us of that period. If he lived today, he would undoubtedly emphasise different aspects of the virtues and their application. But there is much in this little book that reminds us of the constant teaching of the masters of the spiritual life, going back to the Desert Fathers (themselves always the favourite reading of St Philip). The maxims are full of sound common sense: 'It is well to choose some good devotion and to stick to it.'; 'Men are generally the carpenters of their own crosses'; 'Not everything which is better in itself, is better for each man in particular'. He also reminds us of things we might have forgotten: 'Excessive sadness seldom springs from any other source than pride'; 'To pray well requires the whole man'; 'He is perfect in the school of Christ who despises being despised'; 'Give me ten men really detached from the world, and I have the heart to believe I could convert the world with them.'

Some readers might well imagine that the last maxim was the work of St Ignatius—the two saints knew each other well and admired each other's apostolate. Both were canonised on the same day. 1995 marked the fourth centenary of St Philip's death, but his voice still rings out: 'The time to do good is not finished yet!'

James Tolhurst DD

January

1. Well! When shall we have a mind to begin to do good?

2. *Nulla dies sine linea.*[*] Do not let a day pass without some good during it.

3. We must not be behind time in doing good; for death will not be behind his time.

4. Happy is the youth, because he has time before him to do good.

5. It is well to choose some one good devotion, and to stick to it, and never to abandon it.

6. He who wishes for anything but Christ, does not know what he wishes; he who asks for anything but Christ, does not know what he is asking; he who works, and not for Christ, does not know what he is doing.

7. Let no-one wear a mask,[†] otherwise he will do ill; and if he has one, let him burn it.

---

[*] Literally 'no day without its line', therefore practice makes perfect (from Pliny).
[†] This refers to the masks worn at Carnival.

8. Spiritual persons ought to be equally ready to experience sweetness and consolation in the things of God, or to suffer and keep their ground in dryness of spirit and devotion, and for as long as God pleases, without their making any complaint about it.

9. God has no need of men.

10. If God be with us, there is no-one else left to fear.

11. He who wishes to be perfectly obeyed, should give but few orders.

12. A man should keep himself down, and not busy himself in *mirabilibus super se* (in marvels beyond his power).

13. Men should often renew their good resolutions, and not lose heart because they are tempted against them.

14. The name of Jesus, pronounced with reverence and affection, has a kind of power to soften the heart.

15. Obedience is a short cut to perfection.

16. They who really wish to advance in the way of God, must give themselves up into the hands of their superiors always and in everything; and

they who are not living under obedience must subject themselves of their own accord to a learned and discreet confessor, whom they must obey in the place of God, disclosing to him with perfect freedom and simplicity the affairs of their soul, and they should never come to any resolution without his advice.

17. There is nothing which gives greater security to our actions, or more effectively cuts the snares the devil lays for us, than to follow another person's will, rather than our own, in doing good.

18. Before a man chooses his confessor, he ought to think well about it, and pray about it also; but when he has once chosen, he ought not to change, except for most urgent reasons, but put the utmost confidence in his director.

19. When the devil has failed in making a man fall, he puts forward all his energies to create distrust between the penitent and the confessor, and so little by little he gains his end at last.

20. Let persons in the world sanctify themselves in their own houses, for neither the court, professions, or labour, are any hindrance to the service of God.

21. Obedience is the true holocaust which we sacrifice to God on the altar of our hearts.

22. In order to be really obedient, it is not enough to do what obedience commands, we must do it without reasoning upon it.

23. Our Blessed Lady ought to be our love and our consolation.

24. The good works which we do of our own will are not so meritorious as those that are done under obedience.

25. The most beautiful prayer we can make, is to say to God, 'As Thou knowest and willest, O Lord, so do with me.'

26. When tribulations, infirmities, and contradictions come, we must not run away in a fright, but vanquish them like men.

27. It is not enough to see that God wishes the good we aim at, but that He wishes it through our instrumentality, in our manner and in our time; and we may come to discern all this by true obedience.

28. In order to be perfect, we must not only obey and honour our superiors; we must honour our equals and inferiors also.

29. In dealing with our neighbour, we must assume as much pleasantness of manner as we can, and by this affability win him to the way of virtue.

30. A man who leads a common life under obedience, is more to be esteemed than one who does great penance after his own will.

31. To mortify one passion, no matter how small, is a greater help in the spiritual life than many abstinences and fasts.

February

1. He who wishes to be wise without true Wisdom, or saved without the Saviour, is not well, but sick—is not wise, but a fool.

2. Devotion to the Blessed Virgin is actually necessary, because there is no better means of obtaining God's graces than through His most holy mother.

3. A man should force himself to be obedient, even in little things which appear of no moment; because he will thus render the practice of obedience in matters easy to himself.

4. He who always acts under obedience may rest assured that he will not have to give an account of his actions to God.

5. Perfection does not consist in such outward things as shedding tears and the like, but in true and solid virtues.

6. Tears are no sign that a man is in the grace of God, neither must we infer that one who weeps when he speaks of holy and devout things necessarily lives a holy life.

7. Cheerfulness strengthens the heart and makes us persevere in a good life; therefore the servant of God ought always to be in good spirits.

8. When a man is freed from a temptation or any other distress, let him take great care to show fitting gratitude to God for the benefit he has received.

9. We must accept the adversities which God sends us without reasoning too much upon them, and we must take for granted that it is the best thing which could happen to us.

10. We must always remember that God does everything well, although we may not see the reason for what He does.

11. Everyone ought to give in readily to the opinion of another, and to argue in favour of another and against himself, and take things in good part.

12. There is nothing more to the purpose for exciting a spirit of prayer, than the reading of spiritual books.

13. Let a man frequent the holy Sacraments, go to sermons, and be often reading the lives of Saints.

14. Let a man always think that he has God before his eyes.

15. When a man is in an occasion of sin, let him look what he is doing, get himself out of the occasion, and avoid the sin.

16. There is nothing good in this world: *Vanitas vanitatum et omnia vanitas.**

17. We must die at last.

18. Beginners in religion ought to exercise themselves principally in meditation on the Four Last Things.†

19. He who does not go down into hell while he is alive, runs a great risk of going there after he is dead.

20. The greatest help of perseverance in the spiritual life is the habit of prayer, especially under the direction of our confessor.

21. There is nothing the devil fears so much, or so much tries to hinder, as prayer.

22. An excellent method of preserving ourselves from relapsing into serious faults, is to say every evening, 'Tomorrow I may be dead.'

---

* Vanity of vanities, all is vanity. (*Ecclesiastes 1:2*)
† Death, Judgement, Hell, Heaven.

23. A man without prayer is an animal without the use of reason.

24. The religious state is indeed the highest, but it is not suitable for all.

25. A most excellent means of learning how to pray, is to acknowledge ourselves unworthy of such a benefit, and to put ourselves entirely into the hand of the Lord.

26. The true preparation for prayer consists in the exercise of mortification; for he who wishes to give himself up to prayer without mortification, is like a bird wishing to fly before it is fledged.

27. We can never arrive at the contemplative life, if we do not first exercise ourselves laboriously in the active life.

28. We must first exercise the spirit which God gives us in prayer, and follow that; so that when, for example, it inclines us to meditate on the Passion, we must not wish to meditate on some other mystery.

29. When a person goes to communion, he ought to follow the same spirit he had in prayer, and not be casting about for new meditations.

March

1. We must never pray for a favour for any one, except conditionally, saying, 'If it please God', or the like.

2. When a spiritual person feels a great calmness of mind in asking anything of God, it is a good sign that God either has granted it or will do so shortly.

3. A man ought never to think he has done any good, or rest contented with any degree of perfection he may have attained, because Christ has given us the type of our perfection, in putting before us the perfection of the Eternal Father. Be ye perfect even as your heavenly Father is perfect. (*Matthew 5:48*)

4. The sweetness which some experience in prayer, is milk which our Lord gives as a relish to those who are just beginning to serve him.

5. To leave our prayer when we are called to do some act of charity for our neighbour, is not really a quitting of prayer, but leaving Christ for Christ, that is depriving ourselves of spiritual sweetness in order to gain souls.

6. It is good for a man to go from prayer rather with an appetite and desire to return to it, than satiated and weary.

7. The wisdom of the Scriptures is learned rather by prayer than by study.

8. A diligent charity in ministering to the sick, is a quick way to the acquisition of perfect virtue.

9. Let women remain indoors, and look after their families, and not be desirous of going into public.

10. We must pray incessantly for the gift of perseverance.

11. We must not leave off our prayers because of distractions and restlessness of mind, although it seems useless to go on with them. He who perseveres for the whole of his accustomed time, gently recalling his mind to the subject of his prayer, merits greatly.

12. If in times of dryness in prayer we make acts of humility, self-knowledge, protestations of our own inability to help ourselves, and petitions for God's assistance, all this is real and substantial prayer.

13. The best remedy for dryness of spirit, is to picture ourselves as beggars in the presence of God and the saints, and like a beggar, to go first to one Saint, then to another, to ask a spiritual alms of them with the same earnestness as a poor fellow in the streets would ask an alms of us.

14. We may ask a spiritual alms even corporally, by going first to the Church of one Saint, and then to the Church of another, to make our petition.

15. Without prayer, a man will not persevere long in spirituality; we must have recourse to this most powerful means of salvation every day.

16. If young men wish to protect themselves from all danger of impurity, let them never retire to their own rooms immediately after dinner, either to read or write, or do anything else; but let them remain in conversation, because at that time the devil is wont to assault us with more than usual vehemence, and this is that demon which is called in Scripture the noon-day demon, and from which holy David prayed to be delivered. (*Psalm 91:6*)

17. If young men would preserve their purity, let them avoid bad company.

18. Let them also avoid nourishing their bodies delicately.

19. It is God's custom to interweave human life with a trouble and a consolation, at least of an inferior sort, alternately.

20. Young men should be very careful to avoid idleness.

21. When fathers have given their sons a good education, and put everything clearly and distinctly in train for them, the sons who succeed them, and continue to follow the road marked out for them, will have the advantage of seeing their family persevere in holy ways, and in the fear of God.

22. In order to preserve their purity, young men should frequent the Sacraments, and especially confession.

23. We must never trust ourselves, for it is the devil's way first to get us to feel secure, and then to make us fall.

24. We ought to fear and fly temptations of the flesh, even in sickness, and in old age itself, aye, and so long as we can open and shut our eyelids, for the spirit of incontinence gives no truce either to place, time, or person.

25. Our sweet Christ, the Word Incarnate, has given Himself to us for every thing that was necessary for us, even to the hard and ignominious death upon the cross.

26. One of the most efficacious means of keeping ourselves chaste, is to have compassion for those who fall through their frailty, and never to boast in the least of being free, but with all humility to acknowledge that whatever we have is from the mercy of God.

27. To be without pity for other men's falls, is an evident sign that we shall fall ourselves shortly.

28. In the matter of purity there is no greater danger than not fearing the danger: when a man does not distrust himself, and is without fear, it is all over with him.

29. We need to pray for the grace to love Jesus not out of fear but out of love.

30. In order to begin well, and to finish better, it is quite necessary to hear mass every day, unless there be some lawful hindrance in the way.

31. A most excellent means of keeping ourselves pure, is to lay open all our thoughts, as soon as possible, to our confessor with the greatest sincerity, and keep nothing hidden in ourselves.

April

1. To acquire and preserve the virtue of chastity, we have need of a good and experienced confessor.

2. Let a man who desires the first place take the last.

3. As soon as a man feels that he is tempted, he should fly to God, and devoutly utter that ejaculation which the fathers of the desert so much esteemed: *Deus in adjutorium meum intende; Domine ad adjuvandum me festina*: or that verse, *Cor mundum crea in me Deus*.[*]

4. When sensual thoughts come into the mind, we ought immediately to make use of our minds, and fix them instantaneously upon something or other, no matter what.

5. Never say, 'What great things the Saints do', but, 'What great things God does in His Saints.'

6. In the warfare of the flesh, only cowards gain the victory; that is to say, those who fly.

---

[*] O God, come to my aid; O Lord make haste to help me; a pure heart create in me, O God.

7. We should be less alarmed for one who is tempted in the flesh, and who resists by avoiding the occasions, than for one who is not tempted and is not careful to avoid the occasions.

8. When a person puts himself in an occasion of sin, saying, 'I shall not fall, I shall not commit it', it is an almost infallible sign that he will fall, and with all the greater damage to his soul.

9. It is a most useful thing to say often, and from the heart, 'Lord, do not put any confidence in me, for I am sure to fall if Thou dost not help me.' or, 'O my Lord, look for nothing but evil from me.'

10. In temptation we ought not to say, 'I will do', 'I will say', for it is a species of presumption and self confidence; we ought rather to say with humility, 'I know what I ought to do, but I do not know what I shall do.'

11. The stench of impurity before God and the angels is so great, that no stench in the world can equal it.

12. We must not trust in ourselves, but take the advice of our spiritual father, and recommend ourselves to everybody's prayers.

13. We must avoid lies as we would a pestilence.

14. When we go to confession, we should accuse
ourselves of our worst sins first, and of those
things which we are most ashamed of, because
by this means we put the devil to greater
confusion, and reap more fruit from our
confession.

15. One of the very best means of obtaining humility, is sincere and frequent confession.

16. In trying to get rid of bad habits, it is of the
greatest importance not to put off going to confession after a fall, and also to keep to the same
confessor.

17. In visiting the dying we should not say many
words to them, but rather help them by praying
for them.

18. A sick man should make God a present of his
will; and if it turns out that he has to suffer for a
long time, he must submit to the Divine Will.

19. The sick man must not fear when he is tempted
to lose confidence, for if he has sinned, Christ
has suffered and paid for him.

20. Let the sick man enter into the Side of Jesus and
His most holy Wounds; let him not be afraid, but
combat manfully, and he will come forth
victorious.

21. The true way to advance in holy virtues, is to persevere in a holy cheerfulness.

22. The cheerful are much easier to guide in the spiritual life than the melancholy.

23. Those who wish to enter upon the religious life, should first of all mortify themselves for a long time, and particularly mortify their will in things to which they have the greatest repugnance.

24. Excessive sadness seldom springs from any other source than pride.

25. Charity and cheerfulness, or charity and humility, should be our motto.

26. It is very necessary to be cheerful, but we must not on that account give in to frivolity.

27. Frivolity incapacitates a person from receiving any additional spirituality from God.

28. Frivolity also roots up the little a man may have already acquired.

29. At table, especially where there are guests, we ought to eat every kind of food, and not say, I like this, and I do not like that.

30. Human language cannot express the beauty of a soul which dies in a state of grace.

May

1. If a man finds it very hard to forgive injuries, let him look at a crucifix, and think that Christ has shed all His Blood for him, and not only forgave His enemies, but prayed the Eternal Father to forgive them also .

2. Let him remember also that when he says the *Pater Noster* every day, instead of asking pardon for his sins, he is calling down vengeance upon them.

3. Men are generally the carpenters of their own crosses.

4. Let us concentrate ourselves so completely in the divine love, and enter so far into the living fountain of wisdom through the wounded Side of our Incarnate God, that we may deny ourselves and our self love, and so be unable to find our way out of that Wound again.

5. We must not give up praying and asking, because we do not get what we ask all at once.

6. He who is unable to spend a long time together in prayer, should often lift up his mind to God by ejaculations.

7. We must often remember what Christ said, that not he who begins, but he that perseveres to the end, shall be saved.

8. We ought to abhor every kind of affectation, whether in talking, dressing, or anything else.

9. When a scrupulous person has once made up his mind that he has not consented to a temptation, he must not reason that matter over again to see whether he has really consented or not, for the same temptations often return by making this sort of reflections.

10. If those who are molested by scruples wish to know whether they have consented to suggestion or not, especially in thoughts, they should see whether, during the temptation, they have always had a lively love of the virtue opposed to the vice in respect of which they were tempted, and hatred of that same vice, and this is mostly a good proof that they have not consented.

11. The scrupulous should remit themselves always and in everything to the judgement of their confessor, and accustom themselves to have a contempt of their own scruples.

12. Scruples are an infirmity which will make a truce with a man, but very rarely peace; humility alone comes off conqueror over them.

13. Even in bodily indispositions spiritual remedies are the most helpful.

14. As much love as we give to creatures, just so much we steal from the Creator.

15. Penitents ought never to force their confessor to give them leave to do any thing against his inclination.

16. He who has the slightest taint of avarice about him, will never make the least advance in virtue.

17. Avarice is the pest of the soul.

18. Experience shows that men given to carnal sins are converted sooner than those who are given to avarice.

19. He who wishes for goods will never have devotion.

20. All sins are highly displeasing to God, but above all sensuality and avarice, which are very difficult to cure.

21. We must always pray God not to let the spirit of avarice domineer over us, but that we may live detached from the affections of this world.

22. If we find nothing in the world to please us, we ought to be pleased by this very discovery.

23. He who wishes to attain to perfection must have no attachment to any thing.

24. It is a good thing to leave the world and our possessions to serve God, but it is not enough.

25. The greatness of our love of God must be tested by the desire we have of suffering for his love.

26. Let us strive after purity of heart, for the Holy Spirit dwells in candid and simple minds.

27. The Holy Spirit is the master of prayer, and causes us to abide in continual peace and cheerfulness, which is a foretaste of Paradise.

28. If we wish the Holy Spirit to teach us how to pray, we must practise humility and obedience.

29. The fruit we ought to get from prayer, is to do what is pleasing to the Lord.

30. A virtuous life consists in mortifying vices, sins, bad thoughts, and evil affections, and in exercising ourselves in the acquisition of holy virtues.

31. Let us be humble and keep ourselves down: Obedience! Humility! Detachment!

June

1. The love which our Blessed Lady had for God was so great, that she suffered keenly through her desire of union with Him; hence the Eternal Father, to console her, sent her His only and beloved Son.

2. If you wish to come where I am going, that is, to glory, you must come this road, that is, through thorns.

3. Before communion, we ought to exercise ourselves in many acts of virtue.

4. Prayer and communion are not to be made or desired for the sake of the devotion we feel in them, for that is seeking self, and not God; but we must be frequent in both the one and the other in order to become humble, obedient, gentle, and patient.

5. When we see these virtues in a man, then we know that he has really gathered the fruit of prayer and of communion.

6. Our sweet Jesus, through the excess of His love and liberality, has left Himself to us in the Most Holy Sacrament.

7. Let all go to the Eucharistic table with a great desire for that Sacred Food. *Sitientes! Sitientes!**

8. To feel any displeasure because we are refused the Communion, is a sign of hardness, pride, and a want of mortification.

9. Those who are going to Communion should prepare themselves for more temptations than usual, for the Lord will not have us stand idle.

10. It is a good thing, during the week that follows our Communion day† to do something more than usual; for example, to say five *Our Fathers* and *Hail Marys* with our arms extended, or an extra rosary.

11. It is not a good thing to load ourselves with many spiritual exercises; it is better to undertake a little, and go on with it; for if the devil can persuade us to omit an exercise once, he will easily get us to omit it the second time, and the third, until at last all our pious practices will melt away.

---

* Thirsting!
† This was before the practice of daily Communion and was considered advanced in its day.

12. We must take care of little faults; for he who once begins to go back[*] and to make light of such defects, brings a sort of grossness over his conscience, and then goes wrong altogether.

13. The servant of God ought to seek knowledge, but never to show it or make a parade of it.

14. Let us always go to confession with sincerity, and take this as our rule—Never out of human respect to conceal anything from our confessor, however inconsiderable it may be.

15. He who conceals a grave sin in confession, is completely in the devil's hands.

16. Penitents should not generally change their confessors, nor confessors be forward to receive the penitents of others; a few particular cases excepted.

17. When a person who has been living a spiritual life for a long time falls into a serious fault, there is no better way of raising him up again than by exhorting him to manifest his fall to any pious friend with whom he has a particular intimacy: and God will reconduct him to his first estate for the sake of his humility.

[*] cf. Sirach 19:1.

18. For young men to make sure of persevering, it is absolutely necessary that they should avoid wicked companions, and be familiar with good ones.

19. In the spiritual life there are three degrees: the first may be called the animal life; this is the life of those who run after sensible devotion, which God generally gives to beginners, to allure them onwards by that sweetness to the spiritual life, just as an animal is drawn on by a sensible object.

20. The second degree may be called the human life; this is the life of those who do not experience any sensible sweetness, but by the help of virtue combat their own passions.

21. The third degree may be called the angelic life; this is the life which they come to, who, having been exercised for a long time in the taming of their own passions, received from God a quiet, tranquil, and almost angelic life, even in this world, feeling no trouble or repugnance in anything.

22. Of these three degrees it is well to persevere in the second, because the Lord will grant the third in His own good time.

23. We must not be too ready to trust young men who have great devotion; we must wait till their wings are grown, and then see what sort of a flight they make.

24. Outward mortifications are a great help towards the acquisition of interior mortification and the other virtues.

25. He who cannot put up with the loss of his honour, can never make any advance in spiritual things.

26. It is generally better to give the body rather too much food than rather too little; for the too much can be easily subtracted, but when a man has injured his constitution by the too little, it is not so easy to get right again.

27. The devil has a crafty custom of sometimes urging spiritual persons to penances and mortifications, in order that by going indiscreet lengths in this way, they may so weaken themselves as to be unable to attend to good works of greater importance; or be so intimidated by the sickliness they have brought upon themselves as to abandon their customary devotions, and at last turn their backs on the service of God.

28. Those who pay a moderate attention to the mortification of their bodies, and direct their main intention to mortify the will and understanding, even in matters of the slightest moment, are more to be esteemed than they who give themselves up exclusively to corporal penances.

29. We ought to desire to do great things for the service of God, and not content ourselves with a moderate goodness, but wish, if it were possible, to surpass in sanctity and love even St Peter and St Paul.

30. Even though a man may be unable to attain such a height of sanctity, he ought to desire it, so as to do at least in desire what he cannot carry out in effect.

July

1. We ought to make no account of abstinences and fasts, when there is self-will in the matter.

2. Our Blessed Lady is the dispenser of all the favours which the goodness of God concedes to the sons of Adam.

3. In seeking for counsel it is necessary sometimes to hear what our inferiors think, and to recommend ourselves to their prayers.

4. A man ought never to say one word in his own praise, however true it may be; no, not even in a joking way.

5. Whenever we do a good work, and somebody else takes the credit for it, we ought to rejoice, and acknowledge it as a gift from God. Anyhow, we ought not to be sorry, because if others diminish our glory before men, we shall recover it with all the more honour before God.

6. Let us pray God, if He gives us any virtue or any gift, to keep it hidden even from ourselves, that we may preserve our humility, and not take occasion of pride because of it.

7. We ought not to publish or manifest to everyone the inspirations which God sends us, or the favours He grants us. *Secretum meum mihi! Secretum meum mihi!** (*Isaiah 24:16*)

8. In order to avoid all risk of vain-glory, we ought to make some of our particular devotions in our own rooms, and never seek for sweetnesses and sensible consolations in public places.

9. The true medicine to cure us of pride, is to keep down and thwart touchiness of mind.

10. When a man is reproved for anything, he ought not to take it too much to heart, for we often commit a greater fault by our sadness than by the sin for which we are reproved.

11. They who when they have got a little devotion think they are someone great, are only fit to be laughed at.

12. Humility is the true guardian of chastity.

13. When a man has fallen, he ought to acknowledge it in some such way as this: 'Ah! if I had been humble I should not have fallen.'

---

* My secret to myself!

14. We ought to be pleased to hear that others are advancing in the service of God, especially if they are our relations or friends; and we ought to rejoice that they share in whatever spiritual good we may have ourselves.

15. In order the better to gain souls, in visiting the sick, we ought to imagine that what we do for the sick man we are doing to Christ Himself; we shall thus perform this work of mercy with more love and greater spiritual profit.

16. He whose health will not permit him to fast in honour of Christ and our Blessed Lady, will please them much more by giving some more alms than usual.

17. Nothing is more dangerous for beginners in the spiritual life, than to wish to play the master, and to guide and convert others.

18. Beginners should look after their own conversion and be humble, lest they should fancy they had done some great thing, and so should fall into pride.

19. If we wish to help our neighbour, we must reserve neither place, hour, or season, for ourselves.

20. Avoid every kind of singularity, for it is generally the hotbed of pride, especially spiritual pride.

21. A man must not, however, abstain from doing a good work merely to get out of the way of a temptation to vain-glory.

22. The love of God makes us do great things.

23. We may distinguish three kinds of vain-glory; the first we may call mistress; that is, when vain-glory goes before our works, and we work for the sake of it; the second we may call companion; that is, when a man does not do a work for the sake of vain-glory, but feels complacency in doing it; the third we may call servant; that is, when vain-glory rises in our work, but we instantly repress it. Above all things never let vain-glory be mistress.

24. When vain-glory is companion, it does not take away our merit; but perfection requires that it should be servant.

25. He who works purely for the love of God, desires nothing but His honour, and thus is ready in every thing either to act or not to act, and that not in indifferent matters only, but even in good ones; and he is always resigned to the Will of God.

26. The Lord grants in a moment what we may have been unable to obtain in dozens of years.

27. To obtain perfectly the gift of humility, four things are required: to despise the world, to despise no person, to despise one's self, to despise being despised.

28. Perfection consists in leading captive our own will, and in playing the king over it.

29. A man ought to mortify his understanding in little things, if he wishes easily to mortify it in great ones, and to advance in the way of virtue.

30. Without mortification nothing can be done.

31. We ought to hope for and love the glory of God by means of a good life.

August

1. St Peter and the other apostles and apostolical men, seeing the Son of God born in poverty, and then living so absolutely without anything, that He had nowhere to lay His Head, and contemplating Him dead and naked on a cross, stripped themselves also of all things, and took the road of the evangelical counsels.

2. Nothing unites the soul of God more closely, or breeds contempt of the world sooner, than being harassed and distressed.

3. In this life there is no purgatory; it is either hell or paradise; for to him who serves God truly, every trouble and infirmity turns into consolations, and through all kinds of trouble he has a paradise within himself even in this world: and he who does not serve God truly, and gives himself up to sensuality, has one hell in this world, and another in the next.

4. To get good from reading the lives of the Saints and other spiritual books, we ought not to read out of curiosity, or skimmingly, but with pauses; and when we feel ourselves warmed, we ought not to pass on, but to stop and follow up the spirit which is stirring in us, and when we feel it no longer then to pursue our reading.

5. To begin and end well, devotion to our Blessed Lady, the Mother of God, is nothing less than indispensable.

6. We have no time to go to sleep here, for paradise was not made for cowards.

7. We must have confidence in God, who is what He always has been, and we must not be disheartened because things turn out contrary to us.

8. Men should not change from a good state of life to another, although it may be better, without taking grave counsel.

9. Let every one stay at home, that is, within himself, and sit in judgement on his own actions, without going abroad to investigate and criticise those of others.

10. The true servants of God endure life and desire death.

11. There is not a finer thing on earth, than to make a virtue of necessity.

12. To preserve our cheerfulness amid sicknesses and troubles, is a sign of a right and good spirit.

13. A man should not ask tribulations of God, presuming on his being able to bear them: there should be the greatest possible caution in this matter, for he who bears what God sends him daily does not do a small thing.

14. They who have been exercised in the service of God for a long time, may in their prayers imagine all sorts of insults offered to them, such as blows, wounds, and the like, and so in order to imitate Christ by their charity, may accustom their hearts beforehand to forgive real injuries when they come.

15. Let us think of Mary, for she is that unspeakable virgin, that glorious lady, who conceived and brought forth, without detriment to her virginity, Him whom the width of the heavens cannot contain within itself.

16. The true servant of God acknowledges no other country but heaven.

17. When God infuses extraordinary sweetnesses into the soul, a man ought to prepare for some serious tribulation or temptation.

18. When we have these extraordinary sweetnesses, we ought to ask of God fortitude to bear whatever He may please to send us, and then to stand very much upon our guard, because there is danger of sin behind.

19. One of the most excellent means of obtaining perseverance is discretion; we must not wish to do everything at once, or become a saint in four days.

20. In our clothes we ought, like St Bernard, to love poverty, but not dirt.

21. He who wishes to advance in spirituality, should never slur over his defects negligently without particular examination of conscience, even independent of the time of sacramental confession.

22. A man should not so attach himself to the means as to forget the end; neither must we give ourselves so much to mortify the flesh as to forget to mortify the brain, which is the chief thing after all.

23. We ought to desire the virtues of prelates, cardinals, and popes but not their dignities.

24. The skin of self-love is fastened strongly on our hearts, and it hurts us to remove it, and the more we get down to the quick the more keen and difficult it is.

25. The first step, which we ought to have taken of ourselves already, we have always in our mind, yet never put it in execution.

26. A man ought to set about putting his good resolutions in practice, and not change them lightly.

27. We must not omit our ordinary devotions for every trifling occasion that may come in the way, such as going to confession on our fixed days, and particularly hearing mass on week-days: if we wish to go out walking, or anything of that sort, let us make our confession and perform our usual exercises first, and then go.

28. It is very useful for whose who minister the word of God, or give themselves up to prayer, to read the works of authors whose names begin with S such as *Saint* Augustine, *Saint* Bernard, &c.

29. Nothing more glorious can happen to a Christian, than to suffer for Christ.

30. There is no surer or clearer proof of the love of God than adversity.

31. When God intends to grant a man any particular virtue, it is His way to let him be tempted to the opposite vice.

September

1. Persons who live in the world should persevere in coming to church to hear sermons, and remember to read spiritual books, especially the lives of the Saints.

2. When temptation comes, a man should remember the sweetness he has had in prayer at other times, and he will thus easily master the temptation.

3. The fervour of spirituality is usually very great in the beginning, but afterwards, the Lord *fingit se longius ire*, makes as though He would go further (*Luke 24:28*): in such a case we must stand firm and not be disturbed, because God is then withdrawing His most holy Hand of sweetnesses, to see if we are strong; and then, if we resist and overcome those tribulations and temptations, the sweetnesses and heavenly consolations return.

4. We ought to apply ourselves to the acquisition of virtue, because in the end the whole terminates in greater sweetness than before, and the Lord gives us back all our favours and consolations doubled.

5. It is easy to infuse a most fervent devotion into others, even in a short time; but the great matter is—to persevere.

6. He who continues in anger, strife, and a bitter spirit, has a taste of the air of hell.

7. To obtain the protection of our Blessed Lady in our most urgent wants, it is very useful to say sixty-three times, after the fashion of a Rosary, 'Virgin Mary, Mother of God, pray to Jesus for me.'

8. When we make this prayer to our Blessed Lady, we give her every possible praise in the least possible compass, because we call her by her name of MARY, and give her those two great titles of Virgin, and Mother of God, and then name JESUS, the fruit of her most pure womb.

9. The things of this world do not remain constantly with us, for if we do not leave them before we actually die, in death at least we all infallibly depart as empty-handed as we came.

10. To pray well requires the whole man.

11. The discipline and other like things ought not to be practised without the leave of our confessor; he who does it of his own will, either hurts his constitution or becomes proud, fancying to himself that he has done some great thing.

12. God takes especial delight in the humility of a man who believes that he has not yet begun to do any good.

13. Before going to confession or taking counsel with our director, it will be very useful to pray for a sincere good will to become a really holy man.

14. He who runs away from one cross, will meet a bigger one on his road.

15. Christ died for sinners; we must take heart therefore, and hope that Paradise will be ours, provided only we repent of our sins, and do good.

16. Never let a sick man set himself to reason with the devil, otherwise he will inevitably be taken in; let him appeal to his spiritual father, of whom the devil stands in mortal fear.

17. He who serves God must do the best he can not to receive the reward of his labours in this world.

18. In giving alms to the poor we must act as good ministers of the Providence of God.

19. He who feels that the vice of avarice has got hold of him, should not wish to observe additional fasts, but to give alms.

20. Perfection cannot be attained without the greatest toil.

21. As soon as we are stripped of the sordid garb of avarice, we shall be clothed with the royal and imperial cloak of the opposite virtue, liberality.

22. Even in the midst of the crowd we can be going on to perfection.

23. Not everything which is better in itself is better for each man in particular.

24. Be devout to the Madonna, keep yourself from sin, and God will deliver you from your evils.

25. If we wish to keep peace with our neighbours, we should never remind any one of his natural defects.

26. We must sometimes bear with little defects in others, as we have against our own will to bear with natural defects in ourselves.

27. Men of rank ought to dress like their equals, and be accompanied by servants, as their state requires, but modesty should go along with it all.

28. We should not be quick at correcting others, but rather to think of ourselves first.

29. Let us think, if we only get to heaven, what a sweet and easy thing it will be there to be always saying with the angels and the saints, *Sanctus, Sanctus, Sanctus.*[*]

30. The best way to prepare for death is to spend every day of life as though it were the last.

[*] Holy, Holy, Holy.

October

1. In passing from a bad state to a good one there is no need of counsel, but in passing from a good one to a better, time, counsel, and prayer must go into the decision.

2. We must continually pray to God for the conversion of sinners, thinking of the joy there is in heaven both to God and the angels in the conversion of each separate sinner.

3. To speak of ourselves without cause, saying 'I have said', 'I have done', incapacitates us for receiving spiritual consolations.

4. We ought to desire to be in such a condition as to want sixpence, and not be able to get it.

5. Let us despise gold, silver, jewels, and all that the blind and cheated world vainly and ignorantly prizes.

6. Let us learn here below to give God the confession of praise which we ought to hope to give Him in heaven above.

7. He who wishes to go to Paradise must be an honest man and a good Christian, and not give heed to dreams.

8. Fathers and mothers of families should bring up their children virtuously, looking at them rather as God's children than their own; and to count life, and health, and all they possess, as loans which they hold from God.

9. In saying the *Pater Noster* we ought to reflect that we have God for our Father in heaven, and so go on making a sort of meditation of it word by word.

10. To make ourselves a stranger to the things of the world, it is a good thing to think seriously of the end of them, saying to ourselves, 'And then? And then?'

11. The devil, who is a most haughty spirit, is never more completely mastered than by humility of heart, and a simple, clear, undisguised manifestation of our sins and temptations to our confessor.

12. We ought not ordinarily to believe prophecies or to desire them, because it is possible there may be many deceits and snares of the devil in them.

13. It is a most useful thing, when we see another doing any spiritual good to his neighbour, to seek by prayer to have a part in that same good which the Lord is working by the hand of another.

14. At communion we ought to ask for the remedy of the vice to which we feel ourselves most inclined.

15. To him who truly loves God, nothing more displeasing can happen than the lack of occasion to suffer for Him.

16. We ought to hate no one, for God never comes where there is no love of our neighbours.

17. We must accept our own death and that of our relations when God shall send it to us, and not desire it at any other time; for it is sometimes necessary that it should happen at that particular moment for the good of our own and their souls.

18. The perfection of a Christian consists in knowing how to mortify himself for the love of Christ.

19. He who desires ecstasies and visions does not know what he is desiring.

20. As for those who run after visions, dreams, and the like, we must lay hold of them by the feet and pull them to the ground by force, lest they should fall into the devil's net.

21. According to the rules of the fathers and ancient monks, whoever wishes to advance in perfection must hold the world in no reputation.

22. There is nothing more displeasing to God, than our being inflated with self-esteem.

23. When a man knows how to break down his own will and to deny his soul what it desires, he has got a good degree in virtue.

24. When a man falls into any bodily infirmity, he must lie and think, and say, 'God has sent me this sickness, because He wishes something of me; I must therefore make up my mind to change my life and become better.'

25. When a man has a tribulation sent him from God, and is impatient, we may say to him, 'You are not worthy that God should visit you; you do not deserve so great a good.'

26. Poverty and tribulations are given us by God as trials of our fidelity and virtue, as well as to enrich us with more real and lasting riches in heaven.

27. Scruples ought to be most carefully avoided, as they disquiet the mind, and make a man melancholy.

28. Let us throw ourselves into the arms of God, and be sure that if He wishes anything of us, He will make us good for all He desires us to do for Him.

29. Nothing helps a man more than prayer.

30. Idleness is a pestilence to a Christian man; we ought always therefore to be doing something, especially when we are alone in our rooms, lest the devil should come in and catch us idle.

31. We ought always to be afraid, and never put any confidence in ourselves; for the devil assaults us on a sudden, and darkens our understanding; and he who does not live in fear is overcome in a moment, because he has not the help of the Lord.

November

1. The great thing is to become Saints.

2. In order to enter Paradise we must be well justi-
   fied and well purified.

3. Let the young man look after the flesh, and the
   old man after avarice, and we shall all be saints
   together.

4. Where there is no great mortification there is no
   great sanctity.

5. The sanctity of a man lies in the breadth of three
   fingers (the forehead), that is to say, in mortifying the understanding, which would delight in
   the powers of its own reasoning.

6. He who really wishes to become a saint must
   never defend himself, except in a few rare cases,
   but always acknowledge himself in fault, even
   when what is alleged against him is untrue.

7. What we know of the virtues of the Saints is the
   least part of them.

8. The relics of the Saints ought to be venerated, and we may laudably keep them in our room; but it is not well unless for some grave occasion to wear them on our persons, because it will often happen then that they are not treated with all the respect which is becoming.

9. The old patriarchs possessed riches, and had wives and children, but they lived without defiling their affections with these things, although they possessed them, because they only allowed themselves the use of them, and were ready to abandon them in whatever way the majesty of God might require of them.

10. We ought to pray God persistently to increase in us every day the light and heat of His goodness.

11. It is an old custom with the servants of God always to have some little prayers ready, and to be darting them up to heaven frequently during the day, lifting their minds to God from out of the filth of this world. He who adopts this plan will get great fruit with little pains.

12. Tribulations, if we bear them patiently for the love of God, appear bitter at first, but they grow sweet, when one gets accustomed to the taste.

13. The man who loves God with a true heart, and prizes Him above all things, sometimes sheds floods of tears at prayer, and has an abundance of favours and spiritual feelings coming upon him with such vehemence, that he is forced to cry out, 'Lord! let me be quiet!'

14. But a man ought not to seek for these sweetnesses and sensible devotions forcibly, for he will be easily deluded by the devil, and will run a risk of injuring his health.

15. When the soul lies resignedly in the hands of God, and is contented with the divine pleasure, it is in good hands, and has the best security that good will happen to it.

16. To be entirely conformed and resigned to the divine Will, is truly a road in which we cannot get wrong, and is the only road which leads us to taste and enjoy that peace which sensual and earthly men know nothing of.

17. Resignation is all in all to the sick man; he ought to say to God, 'Lord, if You want me, here I am, although I have never done any good: do with me what You will.

18. Never make a noise of any sort in church, except for the greatest necessity.

19. Patience is necessary for the servant of God, and we must not be distressed at trouble, but wait for the consolation.

20. When seculars have once chosen their secular state, let them persevere in it, and in the devout exercises which they have begun, and in the works of charity, and they shall have contentment at their death.

21. The vocation to the religious life is one of the great benefits which the Mother of God obtains from her Son for those who are devoted to her.

22. There is nothing more dangerous in the spiritual life, than to wish to rule ourselves after our own way of thinking.

23. Among the things we ought to ask of God, is perseverance in well doing and in serving the Lord; because, if we only have patience, and persevere in the good life we have begun to lead, we shall acquire a most eminent degree of spirituality.

24. He is perfect in the school of Christ who despises being despised, rejoices in self-contempt, and accounts himself to be very nothingness.

25. The way which God takes with the souls that love Him, by allowing them to be tempted and to fall into tribulations, is a true espousal between Himself and them.

26. In temptations of the flesh, a Christian ought to have immediate recourse to God, make the sign of the cross over his heart three times, and say, 'Christ, Son of God, have mercy on me.'

27. As to temptations, some are mastered by flying from them, some by resisting them, and some by despising them.

28. In order to acquire prudence, and to make a good judgement, we must have lived long and been intimate with many people.

29. It is a great perfection in a heart when it is discreet, and does not overstep the limits of convenience and what is befitting.

30. We must seek Christ where Christ is not, that is, in crosses and tribulations, in which truly He is not now, but we shall find Him in glory by this road.

December

1. Frequent confession is the cause of great good to the soul, because it purifies it, heals it, and confirms it in the service of God: we ought not therefore to omit confession on our fixed days for any business whatsoever; but go to confession first, and to business afterwards, and the first will help the last.

2. When we go to confession, we ought to persuade ourselves to find Jesus Christ in the person of our confessor.

3. Give me ten men really detached from the world, and I have the heart to believe I could convert the world with them.

4. He who communicates often, as he ought to do, brings forth good fruit, the fruit of humility, the fruit of patience, the fruit of all the virtues.

5. Penitents ought not to go to confession for temporal ends, to get alms and the like.

6. We ought to make no account of an immodest person, notwithstanding that he may possess other virtues.

7. The Holy Spirit says of prelates and pastors, He who hears and obeys his superiors, hears and obeys Me, and he who despises them, despises and disobeys Me.

8. If the servant of God would trace his steps safely through so many snares scattered in every place, he should have our Blessed Lady as his mediatrix with her Son.

9. The sick man may desire to get well, provided he seals his desire always with an 'If it please God', 'If it is good for my soul'; for we can do many good things in health, which sickness hinders us from doing.

10. In sickness we ought to ask God to give us patience, because it often happens, that when a man gets well, he not only does not do the good he proposed to do when he was sick, but he multiplies his sins and his ingratitude.

11. The mole is a blind rat, which always stays in the ground; it eats earth, and hollows it out, but is never satisfied with it: so is the avaricious man or woman.

12. Penitents should never make vows without the advice of their spiritual fathers.

13. If we do make such vows, it is best to make them conditionally: for example, 'I make a vow to have two masses said on St Lucy's day, with this bargain, *'If I can, if I do not forget it,* because if I do not remember it I do not wish to be bound.'

14. When a man has to buy anything, he ought not to do so because he is moved by an attachment to the thing, but from want and necessity; for it will never do to buy attachments.

15. Certain little voluntary attachments of self-love must be cut through, and then we must dig round them, and then remove the earth, till we get down deep enough to find the place where they are rooted and interlaced together.

16. A person must be ready to endure, when through a virtuous motive he is mortified by others, and even when God permits him to be in bad odour with others, and regarded and driven away as an infected sheep.

17. Our enemy the devil, who fights with us in order to vanquish us, seeks to disunite us in our houses, and to breed quarrels, dislikes, contests, and rivalries, because while we are fighting with each other, he comes and conquers us, and makes us more securely his own.

18. He who does not think on the benefits he receives from God in this life, and on those greater ones His mercy has prepared in that other life of bliss, does not nourish love to God, but chills and freezes it.

19. If a soul could altogether abstain from venial sins, the greatest pain it could have would be to be detained in this life, so great would its desire be of union with God.

20. In the persecutions which bad men excite against piety and devotion, we must keep our eyes on God, whom we would serve, and on the testimony of a good conscience.

21. How patiently Christ, the King and Lord of heaven and earth, bore with the apostles, enduring at their hands many incivilities and misbeliefs, they being but poor and rough fishermen! How much more ought we to bear with our neighbour, if he treats us with incivility!

22. We must give ourselves to God altogether.

23. God makes all His own the soul that is wholly given to Him.

24. It is a general rule a bad sign when a man has not a particular feeling of devotion on the chief feasts of the year.

25. Let us reflect that the Word left heaven, and stooped to become man for us.

26. Besides pardoning those who persecute us, we ought to feel pity for the delusion they are labouring under.

27. To one who really loves God, there is nothing more harassing or burdensome than life.

28. Let young men be cheerful, and indulge in the recreations proper to their age, provided they keep out of the way of sin.

29. Not to know how to deny our soul its own wishes, is to foment a very hotbed of vices.

30. All created things are liberal, and show the goodness of the Creator. the sun scatters its light, the fire its heat; the tree throws out its arms, which are its branches, and reaches to us the fruit it bears: water, and air, and all nature express liberality of the Creator, and we, who are His lively image, do not represent Him, but through our degenerate manners deny Him in deeds while we are confessing Him with our mouths.

31. The hour is finished—we may say the same of the year; but the time to do good is not finished yet.

The Life of St Philip Neri

1515 Born in Florence on 21 July.

1533 Goes to his uncle Romolo in San Germano.

1535 Travels to Rome where he lives a life of prayer and study and begins a lay apostolate.

1548 Founds the Confraternity of the Holy Trinity for the sanctification of its own members and the care of pilgrims, with Fr Persiano Rosa his spiritual director.

1551 Ordained priest on 23 May and goes to live at St Girolomo della Carità. He begins to give conferences in his room, the origin of the 'Oratory'.

1575 Pope Gregory XIII gives the community the Church of Santa Maria in Vallicella, which St Philip rebuilds and becomes known as the Chiesa Nuova (New Church). The congregation of the Oratory is approved by the Pope on 15 July.

1595 St Philip dies on 26 May.

1622 Canonised (with St Ignatius and St Teresa of Avila).

Cardinal Newman's Prayer to St Philip

Philip, my glorious advocate, teach me to look at all I see around me after thy pattern as the creatures of God. Let me never forget that the same God who made me, made the whole world and all men and all animals that are in it. Gain me the grace to love all God's works for God's sake, and all men for the sake of my Lord and Saviour who has redeemed them by the Cross. And especially let me be tender and compassionate and loving towards all Christians, as my brethren in grace. And do thou, who on earth wast so tender to all, be especially tender to us, and feel for us, bear with us in all our troubles, and gain for us from God, with whom thou dwellest in beatific light, all the aids necessary for bringing us safely to Him and to thee.

(from *Meditations and Devotions*)

Other books from Gracewing

St Philip Neri: The Roman Socrates — *Louis Bouyer*

(translated by Fr Michael Day)

A moving life of the founder of the Oratorian order by the well known French theologian and spiritual writer Louis Bouyer.

Published November 1994   0 85244 299 8

112 pages   £7.99

A Newman Compendium for Sundays & Feastdays

Edited by Fr James Tolhurst

Brings together a reading from John Henry Newman for every Sunday and Feastday in the three-year cycle. Ideal for clergy preparing homilies, or for lay people to use at home.

Published January 1995   0 85244 292 0

240 pages   £9.99

Lightning Source UK Ltd.
Milton Keynes UK
UKOW04f2209070118
315717UK00001B/2/P